GIVEAWAYS

Giveaways

An ABC Book of Loanwords from the Americas

Linda Boyden

University of New Mexico Press
Albuquerque

© 2010 by the University of New Mexico Press
All rights reserved. Published 2010
Printed and bound in China by Oceanic Graphic Printing
Design and composition by Karen Mazur

16 15 14 13 12 11 10   1 2 3 4 5 6 7

Library of Congress Cataloging-in-Publication Data

Boyden, Linda.
 Giveaways : an ABC book of loanwords from the Americas / Linda Boyden.
   p. cm.
  ISBN 978-0-8263-4726-8 (cloth : alk. paper)
  1. English language—Foreign words and phrases—Indian—Juvenile literature.
2. English language—Foreign words and phrases—Hawaiian—Juvenile
literature. 3. Indigenous peoples—America—Language—Juvenile literature. 4.
Indians—Languages—Juvenile literature. 5. Hawaiians—Languages—Juvenile
literature. 6. America—Languages—Juvenile literature. 7. English language—
Alphabet—Juvenile literature. 8. Alphabet books—Juvenile literature. I. Title.
  PE1582.A3B69 2010
  497--dc22

                        2010008317

Dedication

I dedicate this book to all the other weirdly wonderful word geeks: anyone who loves words, their histories and meanings.

I must send a special shout-out to the Kevin Snider Physical Therapy "family" in Anderson, California. During my tedious recovery from knee replacement surgery, they would not let me whine or give up. Thanks (in ABC order, of course!) to Andy, Betsy, Bev, Brett, Cheryl, Jennifer, Kevin, Shane, Stephanie, Stephanie, and Traci.

Last and always, thanks to my family.

Author's Note

I am a word geek. I love some words for their sounds, like *thwart* and *plethora*. Others I love for their meanings, like *imagine* and *if*, and I love, love, love the dictionary. It is loaded with incredible information and cool words like *etymologist*. Etymologists are people who study words, languages, and word histories. They say many languages grow by adopting words from other languages, a.k.a. *loanwords*.

American English is a gigantic stew, simmering with loanwords. One example is *okra*, a vegetable. Both the plant and the word were introduced to the Americas from Africa. Whenever we say okra, we are speaking a word that belongs to two languages.

I wrote this book to share an alphabet of loanwords from the First Peoples of the Americas—North, South, and Central—to celebrate their important contribution to American English. You might think that *squash* is a common English word, and it is, but first it was a word from the Narragansett language. Never heard of the Narragansett language or the Narragansett people? Before European contact in 1492, it is estimated that over two million Native people lived on the North American continent alone, speaking more than three hundred different languages.

canoe

barbeque

opossum

abalone

toboggan

Millions of other Native people lived and spoke hundreds of different languages in South and Central America, too. Today, many Native languages are living languages like English. Many other Indian languages are being revived.

About my title: Giveaways are a tradition among most Native People. We often give gifts to visitors and friends. So from my heart to yours, I give my art and my words and hope you learn something about our weirdly wonderful world.

(A-buh-LOH-nee)

Muwekma Ohlone Nation, *aulon*
To Spanish, *abulones*
To English, abalone

Long ago, and even longer, one of the Native peoples of the northern California coast, the Ohlones of Monterey Bay (now called the Muwekma Ohlone Nation), fished for sea creatures they named *aulon*. In time, Spanish settlers arrived. The Spanish took their word and changed it to *abulones*. Later, American settlers moved in and changed the spelling to abalone.

Despite the differences among these three cultures, they have all savored the delicious meat of the abalone and have created jewelry from its shiny mother-of-pearl shells.

Abalones are sea snails that live off rocky shores near many continents. Their oval, single shells give abalone colorful names—white, pink, black, green, and red. Abalone shells get their color from kelp and the other kinds of seaweed they eat.

Aa Abalone

Bad News: Today, abalone populations are decreasing for various reasons: warming ocean waters, diseases, and predators such as sea otters and humans who overfish. People do so because abalone meat has always been in big demand, but abalones grow slowly. It takes years for them to reach their adult size and to be able to reproduce.

Good News: A recent alternative to overfishing is abalone aquaculture, or underwater farming. In many places around the world abalones are raised on "farms." They are kept in underwater cages and fed kelp cut by the owners. The farmers take only the kelp that they need so the plants keep growing.

Wicked Good News: Many governments and organizations have passed laws to protect abalones. Kids can help, too. Learn what abalone shells look like. If you find some clinging to rocks at low tides, don't try to pry them off. If abalones are cut, they cannot stop themselves from bleeding to death, or they will die waiting for the tide to return them to the sea.

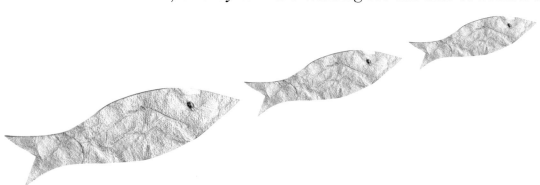

In many ways,
the future of the abalone
rests in our hands.

(BAHR-bi-kyoo)

Taino, *barbakoa*
To Spanish, *barbacòa*
To English, barbecue

On Washington State's Puget Sound, friends from the Coast Salish Nation welcome a journeying dugout canoe club. They are hosting a salmon barbecue, cooking the fish the traditional way on alder sticks. Most people enjoy barbecuing food, but where did this word and custom originate?

In 1492 the Taino people of the Caribbean discovered strangers from a distant world on their shores, Christopher Columbus and his crew. The strangers enjoyed the Taino way of cooking: meat roasted outside on a wooden platform resting on sticks. Later, the strangers introduced *barbakoa* and the custom to the rest of the world.

Today we barbecue food in many ways. Some people use gas or charcoal grills; others dig pits for slow-roasting meat. People barbecue chicken, pork, mutton, beef, fish, and vegetables basted in sweet sauces or spicy marinades.

No matter what is barbecued or how, the results equal the same 4Fs: food, family, friends, and fun!

Bb Barbecue

(kuh-NOO)

From Carib to Arawakan, *canoe*
To English, canoe

Bordering the Pacific Ocean, the coastal lands of the Pacific Northwest were once called "the Canoe Nation." A moist, temperate climate produced rich forests teeming with life, including an eight to ten feet giant tree species, the western red cedar.

Before European contact, the American Indians and the First Nations people of Canada lived on the land and carefully observed and understood it. Some noticed many weirdly wonderful things about the giant cedars: if one had fallen, it was slow to rot; its wood was light, easy to carve and floated on the water—perfect material for seagoing vessels. And so the Canoe Nation came to be.

Time passed and strangers came with different ways of doing things. The days of the Canoe Nation almost ended, but luckily many Native elders preserved the old ways, passing the traditions to the younger generation.

Today, like long ago, many Pacific Northwest Native peoples belong to canoe clubs and carve canoes. Most use modern tools like chain saws, but some prefer to carve with only hand tools: adzes, hatchets, crooked knives and straight knives, chisels, mallets, armored gloves, and, of course, lots of elbow grease!

When a carver finds a proper tree, he or she will imagine or "find" the bottom of the canoe and work their way down, carving away what is not needed. Other team members are pullers. They row the canoe and help to carve it, but must also make their own paddles. Each team must learn the traditional songs and other customs necessary for making a canoe journey.

Carving a canoe, whether the traditional way or with modern tools, takes much time and patience, great skill, and many helping hands. Like a canoe journey itself, canoe carving requires a team to pull together.

(DOU-ich-er)

From N. Iroquoian, probably Mohawk, *tawístawis*
To English, dowitcher

There are two species of sandpipers called dowitchers, the Long-billed and the Short-billed, but both look so similar that for years even scientists were tricked. The best way to tell them apart is to listen: Short-billeds make a *tu-tu* sound while Long-billeds go *keet, keet.*

Every winter, dowitchers migrate south to the coasts of either the Atlantic or Pacific oceans and beyond. Every summer, they return to breed in Alaska or Canada in either the boggy swamplands called *muskegs* or the *taiga* forests that border the tundra plains.

During breeding season, males sing to attract females. Females build round nests on the ground near the water. They lay three or four brownish-greenish eggs that hatch in about three weeks. Both parents share the incubation period. Right after hatching, baby dowitchers can walk and will swim as soon as they are dry. Neither parent feeds the hatchlings, but the males—not the females—stay close by and look after them.

Dd Dowitcher

When you visit a beach, listen and try to tell which dowitcher you hear—a Long-billed or a Short-billed.

(YOO-luh-kon or OO-luh-kon)

Chinook, *ulakun*

To the Chinook Jargon, *eulachon*

To English, eulachon

Eulachon, or candlefish, is a ten inch silver fish of many names: ulakun, hooligan, eulachan, eulichan, ooligan, and oolichan, but scientists call them smelt. Each spring they return to lay their eggs in the coastal rivers of the Pacific Northwest. The areas around the rivers, from Oregon to Canada's British Columbia and on to Alaska, are the homelands of many American Indian nations and First Nation peoples of Canada.

Some people called eulachon the "savior" fish because each spring their return meant fresh food would be back again, too. Although small, 20 percent of the eulachon's body weight is fat. After netting, most are buried, allowed to ripen, then boiled, a process that renders them into nutritious oil as clear as salad oil. They can be eaten with fresh berries, used for frying foods, or used as dipping oil for other kinds of foods.

Some eulachon were not rendered into oil, but were put to a weirdly wonderful use: after drying on racks in the sun, wicks were inserted into each mouth. The fish would then be burned as a candle, and so they earned another name, candlefish!

Long ago, it was easy to catch eulachon because there were so many. Since the mid-1990s, however, both Native people and scientists have become concerned about eulachon's declining numbers. Many suspect this is due to global warming, shrimp trawling, and pollution.

Maybe the little "savior" fish, the eulachon, needs to be saved.

Ee Eulachon

(FAH-nee-LOO-sah) (BAHY-oo)

Choctaw, *fani lusa*, to English
Choctaw, *bayuk*, to French, *bayou*
To English, Fanilusa Bayou

Few Native American languages contain the sound of the letter *f*, but all the words in the name Fanilusa Bayou originated from the Choctaw language: *fani*, or squirrel, *lusa*, black or burnt, and *bayuk*, creek. Some people have had trouble pronouncing Fanilusa, so the bayou is also known as Funny Louis!

Some say long ago two Choctaw men out hunting cornered a squirrel in a hollow tree. They built a fire to smoke it out, but the fire burned the tree to a blackened stump. The squirrel left happy; the hunters, not so much, but that's how the bayou got its name.

Fanilusa Bayou is located in rural La Salle and Catahoula Parishes in Louisiana. Louisiana has approximately 3,500 miles of surface waters because the Mississippi River flows through it from north to south. No one knows exactly how many bayous there are because the river changes. During flood years, new bayous are added, but during droughts, many bayous dry up.

Wetlands such as bayous are vital habitats to hundreds of species, from plants, fish, and birds

to insects, reptiles, and mammals. . . and don't forget, squirrels!

Ff Fanilusa Bayou

(GOO-ee-duhk)

From Puget Salish, *gweduc*
To English, geoduck

I f you stood on a Pacific coast shore, you wouldn't suspect that under your sandy feet might be a hundred-year-old clam, the geoduck. Pronounced GOO-ee-duhk, this clam cannot quack and is not sticky or gooey. The word comes to English from the Puget Salish phrase *gweduc*, which means to "dig deep," something you must do to capture one of these wonderfully weird clams that many people like to eat.

Until they reach adulthood, geoducks are food for marine predators. Despite this, scientists estimate that millions of adult geoducks survive. How does an animal with no teeth, brains, eyes, or ears do that?

First, it is a simple animal, having a shell plus three main parts: body, siphon, and digging foot. To breathe and eat, it raises its siphon, a muscular neck with two openings; one opening takes in water and the geoduck's food, algae, and the other expels waste products.

Second, the geoduck is the ultimate couch potato. When it is young, it gweducs or burrows with its foot vertically down in the sand or gravel. It proceeds slowly, taking about two *years* to dig down two or three *feet*! Once there, the geoduck stays in the same spot, safe from most predators, for the rest of its adult life, which can be very long.

Gg Geoduck

The oldest recorded geoduck lived for over *160* years!

(HOH-gahn)

From Navajo, Dineh, *hooghan*
To English, hooghan or hogan

To the Dineh or Navajo people, a hooghan is more than just a building. It is a place of order and simple beauty, a symbol of long life and happiness. Most modern Navajo families live in homes like yours—apartments, condos, houses, or mobile homes, but many have built a hooghan on their property, too.

There are two styles of hooghans: the male hooghan (see opposite page) is conical, made from forked poles or logs, the chinks filled in with earth that hardens like clay. The entrance must face east to welcome the dawn and honor the Holy People, the Immortals. This style of hooghan is used for sacred and healing ceremonies.

The second type is the female hooghan, built larger and round, or sometimes octagonal. It can be made from poles and earth, stones, railroad ties, or whatever materials the family chooses. Its entrance also faces east. This type of hooghan is where the family gathers to enjoy each other's company and for celebrations.

The hooghan, the place home,
came to the People, the Dineh,
from the *Diyin Dine'é*, the Holy People,
those without change, the Immortals.

Hh Hooghan

Children listen as adults share everyday events or the timeless stories of their Dineh traditions.

To them, the hooghan will always be "the place home."

First Man, *Átsé hastiin*,
    First Woman, *Átsé asdz*,
Coyote, *M'ii*, First Boy, *Átsé ashkii*,
    and First Girl, *Átsé at'ééd*,
Talking God, *Haashch'ééti'í*,
    and Calling God, *Hashch'éoghan*,
these are the Immortals, the Holy People.
The four colors and directions,
    the white light of dawn in the east,
the blue light of midday in the south,
    the yellow light of twilight in the west,
the black of night in the north,
    and the Wind,
these too, are the Immortals,
the Holy People, the *Diyin Dine'é*.

    First Man built the hooghan
from poles of beauty,
from poles of white shell, turquoise,
    abalone and jet, he made it.
The poles were serenaded,
songs were sung to the poles.

    To the east, they sang of the Earth.
To the south, they sang of the mountains.
    To the west, they sang of water.
To the north, they sang to First Man's
medicine bundle, to the jeweled kernels of
    white shell, turquoise, abalone, and jet,
the voices sang, the voices sing.

The Holy People came to this,
the Fourth World, from them came the
Dineh.
To them were given the hooghan,
    the place home, house of dawn,
    house of afterglow, house of rainbows.
To them with the hooghan was also given
    The Blessingway, the *Hózhó*,
the center of every blessing of life,
so they say.

(i-GWAH-nuh)

From Taino, *iguana*
To English, iguana

Don't be tricked: Green iguanas may look like mini-dinosaurs with their spiked ridges and long, swaying tails, but they are 100 percent reptiles. They have internal skeletons, external scales, hatch from eggs, and are cold-blooded (they cannot regulate their body temperature).

Iguanas can be as long as six feet snout to tail and weigh up to eleven pounds. Their natural habitats are the warm, humid climates of Central and South America and the Caribbean Islands, but they have been introduced around the world.

Green iguanas are expert climbers. Their flexible toes and sharp claws grasp almost anything and help them break dangerous falls. They are also excellent swimmers and can stay submerged for up to thirty minutes, swimming not with their legs but with their tails.

Many people think green iguanas would make cool pets, but for most people—and definitely for the iguanas—this is not a good idea. Most iguanas die quickly in captivity because they are fed the wrong diet or their terrariums do not have the proper temperature and humidity. Due to habitat loss and the pet trade, the green iguana is considered a threatened species, which is a message for humans to keep iguanas in the wild.

I i Iguana

(JAG-gwahr)

From Tupi/Guarani, *yaguara*
To Portuguese, *jaguar*
To English, jaguar

The largest of the New World cats, the jaguar lives in Central and South America. For centuries, Native people honored this mighty hunter. In the Maya culture, the jaguar belongs to both the spiritual and physical worlds. In the Aztec Nation a man could earn his way into an elite warrior group called the *Ocelomeh*, or the Society of the Jaguar.

The jaguar is a perfect hunter, with a stocky muscular body (120 to 200 pounds), large head, and powerful jaws. It stalks its prey silently through the forest and then pounces for a quick kill. They are carnivores, and carnivores eat any kind of meat they can find, from mice to deer.

A Weird and Eww! Fact: After bringing down its prey, the jaguar cracks the skull between the ears, piercing the brain with its sharp canine teeth and killing its prey in a single snap. Its original Tupi name, *yaguara*, means "the beast that kills with one bound."

The only dangers jaguars face are from humans. Most countries now have laws against killing jaguars for their beautiful skins, although it is hard to stop illegal poaching. Ranchers who need to protect their cattle or sheep also kill jaguars. However, jaguars are driven to kill livestock because their habitats have been taken for ranchlands.

J j jj Jaguar

Jaguars, the mighty hunters, the national animal of Brazil, deserve a fighting chance to survive.

(kin-i-KUH-nik)

From Delaware Unami, *kələk ˙əní ˙k ˙an*
To English, kinnikinnik

Kinnikinnik is a low-growing evergreen plant with tons of names. Its scientific name combines Greek and Latin words into a real tongue twister, *Arctostaphylos uva-ursi*, that translates as bearberry, one of its English names.

In 1804 when captains Lewis and Clark explored the Louisiana Territory, the Native people they met called the plant by different names, too. To the Chippewa it was known as *sacacommis*; to the Blackfoot, *kakahsiin*; to the Pawnee, *nakasis*. When artist George Catlin painted portraits of Plains tribal members in the 1830s, he was told the plant's name was kinnikinnik, from the original Delaware language.

Native people have and still use kinnikinnik in healing teas or stews, but the word literally means *a mixture* to be smoked or used in smudging ceremonies.

Species of kinnikinnik are also native around the world, so it has *more* names: bear's-grape, chipmunk's apple, crowberry, manzanita, hogberry, mountain laurel, redberry, rapper-dandies, and whortleberry, to name a few.

To the forest animals, kinnikinnik is a year-round food source and winter survival food. They seriously do not care what humans call it.

Kk Kinnikinnik

(LAH-muh)

From Quechua, *llama*
To English, llama

True or False? 25,000 years ago, if you lived in Kansas and you were in your backyard, you would have spotted a herd of llamas?
    Answer: Mostly false. Neither the United States nor humans existed 25,000 years ago, but there were prehistoric llama-like ancestors living in North America.

With the coming of the last ice age, these early llamas probably migrated north into Asia, evolving into the dromedary and Bactrian camels. Others migrated to South America where they became vicuñas (check out the V page) and guanacos.

The Inca Indians of Peru domesticated llamas 6,000 years ago as pack animals in their rugged mountain homes. Today in North America, llamas are popular pack animals too, and are also used for wool, meat, and as guard animals for goats or sheep. Huh?

A herd animal themselves, llamas are truly at home on the range. They eat what the herd eats and require no special housing or care. Gelded male llamas make the best guard llamas. Standing over five feet tall and weighing close to 300 pounds, one guard llama can easily care for a large flock. If a coyote or other predator approaches, the llama sends out an alarm call, which sounds like a NASCAR engine revving up. If the predator doesn't take the hint, the llama will use its secret weapon, cud.

Ll Llama

A Weird and Eww! Fact: Cud is swallowed food stored in one of the llama's three stomachs. When upset enough, the llama regurgitates cud and spits it at the predator...green, smelly cud and lots of it, very quickly. If this doesn't work, llamas definitely deliver a powerful kick. Guard llamas are a humane way to protect sheep and goats from predators.

(meyz)

From Taino, *maisi*
To Spanish, *maiz*
To English, maize

For thousands of years humans have roasted, boiled, popped, or ground maize (corn), but scientists are still studying how and precisely when its ancestor, a wild grass called *teosinte*, was first cultivated. They guess that Native farmers from southern Mexico began growing teosinte 10,000 years ago, although it looked nothing like the plant we know. How did teosinte evolve into modern maize?

Each season, the ancient farmers saved the best teosinte kernels to plant the next season. It took thousands of years and thousands of human hands to change teosinte into our modern types of maize.

From Mexico, maize traveled to South America, thriving from the Andes Mountains to tropical lands. From the Maya, Aztec, Inca, and other civilizations, maize traveled further.

The Anasazi introduced maize to the North American Southwest. Over time, it became a vital food source from the Mississippi River to the Atlantic Ocean. Eventually, maize became a favorite worldwide food.

To the Native people of the Americas, however, maize is a sacred blessing from the Creator. The Cherokee word for maize, *selu*, is translated as both spirit and corn. It is also believed that First Woman, Grandmother Corn, *Ginitsi Selu*, grew from a cornstalk. Many other Indian nations also honor maize as a first woman or first man. Many tribes hold ceremonies each year, such as the Green Corn Dance, to give thanks for the gifts of corn, earth, sun, and rain.

Mm Maize

(nay-nay)

From Hawaiian, *Nēnē*
To English, Nēnē

I n the mountains of many Hawaiian Islands live our planet's most rare geese, the Nēnē. Their survival is a flip-flop tale of good and bad news:

Good News: Before humans discovered Hawaii, the Nēnē lived in a bird paradise, with few predators and plenty to eat.

Bad News: They developed no sense of danger.

Okay News: When Polynesian seafarers arrived, they called the geese Nēnē because of their soft *nay, nay* sounds. The geese were valued for their meat and feathers. Many Nēnē survived by moving further up the mountains.

Worse News: Centuries later, explorers from around the globe moved to Hawaii. More people meant less space for the Nēnē, but worse, animals they brought with them, from cats to mongeese, became Nēnē predators. The Nēnē retreated higher up the mountains.

Wicked Bad News: Higher up meant less food. Also, Nēnē build nests on the ground, so predators can easily feed on the eggs or hatchlings.

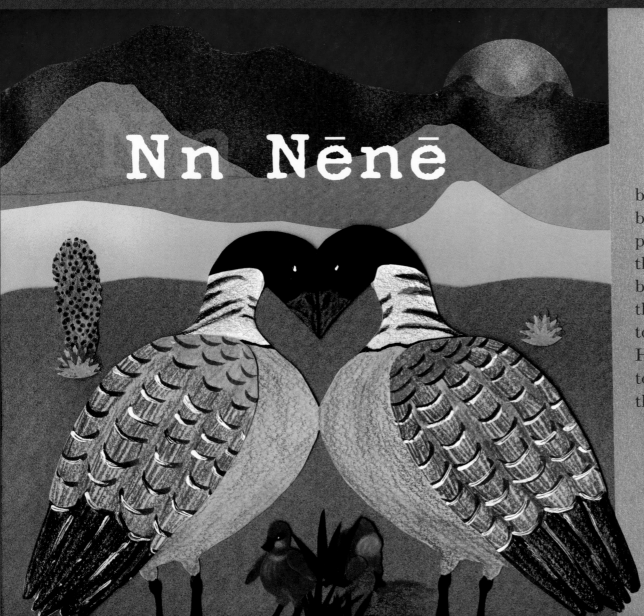

Nn Nēnē

Wicked Good News:
In 1957 the Nēnē became the Hawaii state bird. Scientists captured pairs of adult Nēnē, kept them in safe places for breeding and hatching, and then released them back to the wild. Today laws, Hawaiian residents, and tourists all work to protect the Nēnē.

`( uh-POS-uhm )`

From Powhatan, *apasum* or *aposoum*
To English, opossum or possum

A Cherokee Legend: A Tale of a Lost Tail

Long ago, or so the grandparents said when I was young, Ol' Possum bragged on and on about his tail. He boasted day and night, night and day, until it got so the other animals did a straight about-face when they saw him a-coming. Didn't matter none to Ol' Possum. If nobody was around, why he'd brag to the wind! Finally, *Tsi'stu*, the trickster rabbit himself, decided to teach Ol' Possum a lesson. He called the others together and whispered his plan, then skedaddled to Ol' Possum's house.

"Hey, Ol' Possum, howdy-do?"

"I do fine, but my tail does finer!"

Tsi'stu stopped him right there. "We know, we know, brother! Fact is, your tail is so fine, we're giving a dance to honor it."

Ol' Possum beamed like a new sunflower. Tsi'stu told Ol' Possum to stay home and wait for Cricket, the hairdresser, who would groom his tail even fancier.

By and by, Cricket arrived. She told Ol' Possum to lie still while she trimmed and clipped. Quicker than a snap, Ol' Possum, he fell asleep. When Cricket woke him, Ol' Possum saw a pretty red ribbon around his tail. Cricket told him to let it be until tonight when he could untie it in front of ever'one in the center of the dance circle.

It was hard to wait, but finally it was time to go to the field. Ever'body was there. Tsi'stu clapped for attention. The drum started a round dance and Ol' Possum began, his tail held high, its red ribbon flashy.

When he reached the center, Ol' Possum, he tore off that ribbon! The crowd hushed, but he kept on a-dancing, head higher, eyes closed, until he heard . . . laughter?

Sure enough, they were all laughing and pointing . . . at him? Slowly, Ol' Possum glanced at his tail. What once was bushy-thick fur was now pink and downright naked! Ol' Possum, he was so embarrassed he fell face-down and played dead, which is what all possums do today whenever embarrassed or frightened . . .

all because, long ago, Ol' Possum sure knew how to brag.

Oo Opossum

Possum Facts: Opossums are North America's only marsupials, mammals with pouches.

Weight: 6–15 pounds

Height: 24–33 inches

Description: Long face of white fur, with black eyes, rounded furless ears, pink nose; long pink or yellow prehensile tails (used for grasping); round bodies with black, gray, or silver fur on the top and white on the underbelly; five toes on the front and hind feet, but the inner toes of the hind feet look like thumbs and are clawless.

Habitats: Swamps, forests, lakes, streams, farms, and towns.

Habits: Possums live alone. They move with a waddle-like gait. Nocturnal feeders, they are omnivores, eating most anything from snails and worms to dead animals, vegetables, and pet food.

Weirdly Wonderful Behavior: Like in the Cherokee story, when upset, a possum plays dead. It collapses and becomes coma-like, stiff and hardly breathing, for as long as four hours. Most predators get bored and are tricked into leaving. The possum wakes up and waddles away.

(PAH-goh-nip)

From Shoshonean (the Uto-Aztecan language family, Shoshone, Comanche, Ute, and Paiute), *payinappih*
To English, pogonip

Suzanne Morgan Williams

A full moon rises over a Nevada mountain range. Earlier, weather conditions had been right for a pogonip. When there is enough moisture in the air (humidity) and the temperature is cold enough, tiny needles of ice may form into a cloud, which is the literal translation of the original word, *payinappih*. Instead of regular snow or sleet, an ice storm blasts the land. Some people call the pogonip the "white death" because it is easy to become hopelessly stranded in the freezing blizzard. Breathing in the ice crystals may also damage lungs. However, the storm is over and now all that remains is a shimmering icy wonderland.

Pp Pogonip

(KOH-hog, KWOH-hog, or KWAH-hog)

From Narragansett, *poquauhock*

To English, quahog

* Note: In Rhode Island (roh-DIE-land), ya betta say it "right": KOH-hog

The Native peoples of New England have always harvested the bivalve clam, the quahog, as food, for making jewelry, and also as wampum (check out the W page).

Quahog clams inhabit most Atlantic Ocean shores but have made Rhode Island's Narragansett Bay famous. Its estuary waters, where salt and fresh waters mix, contain the right amount of salt and perfect temperatures for quahogs. However, due to pollutants and excess nutrients, the bay now has some "dead zones," areas of oxygen-poor water. Pollutants hurt sea life, and excess nutrients spur certain algae to grow faster than a speeding computer virus. Algae deplete oxygen from the water and that means less sea life. In a recent Brown University experiment, quahogs, blue mussels, and soft-shell clams were "planted" in some of the dead zones. Surprisingly, only the quahogs survived, and they did because sea stars could not. Why?

A Weird and Ewww! Fact: Sea stars are efficient predators. Their favorite food? Quahogs. Once a sea star snags a quahog, it wraps its five little legs around the quahog's shell. Each leg's hundreds of tiny suction cups pry open the shell. The sea star oozes out a chemical that turns the quahog into a mushy lunch.

Qq Quahog

Good News/ Bad News: The Brown University experiment proved that the quahog's major predator couldn't survive in a dead zone. However, a healthy ocean needs to be an interconnected food chain system. No dead zones allowed.

(ra-KOON)

From Virginia Algonquin/Powhatan, *aroughcun*
To English, raccoon

In 1929 Harriet E. "Petey" Weaver, California's first female park ranger, recorded that raccoons looked at themselves in the still waters of a pond. This surprised many scientists. Until then they believed only dolphins, great apes, and humans could observe themselves in a mirror, but that's not all raccoons can do.

Besides being the #1 Midnight Trash Can Thrashers, raccoons do some weirdly wonderful tricks: some can turn doorknobs, open cans, unlace shoes, watch television and then mimic some of what they see, turn on faucets, and pitch fruit from trees at snarling predators! Raccoons are also extreme vocalists—they growl, hiss, whine, purr, and make more than 200 different sounds.

Six species of raccoons live in North, Central, and South America in many habitats and climates. They are nocturnal, sleeping most days unless extra hungry. Omnivores, raccoons eat many foods: from carrion to frogs, insects, worms, fruit, pet food, and most anything in a trash can.

A popular myth says raccoons wash their food before eating, but recent studies disagree. Raccoons manipulate their food, in water or not. In fact, the Powhatan original name, *aroughcun*, means "he who scratches with his hands." Perhaps raccoons' sensitive paws help them to decide what parts of their food to save and what to throw away.

A raccoon's round eyes, cute furry mask, and cuddly body might make you want one for a pet. This is a seriously bad idea because raccoons can carry a disease called rabies. Abandoned kits (baby raccoons) or injured raccoons need professional help (call a local animal shelter). To be safe, observe them from a distance, and like Ranger Weaver, record their clever antics.

Rr Raccoon

(SKUHNGK)

From Massachusett, *squnck*
To English, skunk

On a moonless night, a common striped skunk has found a hen house door unlocked. After feasting on eggs, a favorite snack, the skunk is cornered by the family dog. The dog may be too young to recognize the skunk's warning signals. Already it has hissed, barred its claws and teeth, and raised its tail, telling the dog to back off or get sprayed with a nasty stink bomb! Skunks make their foul-smelling spray from musk scent glands. They produce only small amounts of musk oil, about enough for five or six uses. It takes up to ten days to make more, so skunks use their spray carefully. Most animals learn very quickly to avoid these small, white striped animals.

From Cherokee, *Sequoyah, sequoia*
To English, Sequoyah, sequoia

In the mountains of Tennessee in the early 1800s, Sequoyah, a crippled Cherokee man who could not read English, created a system of reading and writing for the Cherokee people. He first tried to make a symbol for every Cherokee word, writing them on hundreds of slates of wood. His work made some people angry and jealous. A few burned down Sequoyah's cabin, sending his wooden words up in smoke.

But Sequoyah would not give up. He knew a written system was the only way to save his beautiful Cherokee language. Although frustrated, he rethought his ideas. Instead of drawing a symbol for each Cherokee word, Sequoyah invented a symbol for each sound. By the 1820s, Sequoyah completed his syllabary of 84 symbols. The Cherokee language is still in use today, thanks in great part to Sequoyah.

One of the wonders of nature, the Pacific Coast's giant redwood trees bear his name, though spelled differently, *sequoia*. Sequoyah himself never saw one of these giants, so why did he give the trees his name?

He didn't. No one is 100 percent sure who did, but most researchers agree that it was probably Stephan Endlicher. Was he a good friend of Sequoyah? No. Professor Endlicher was a scientist from Austria, thousands of miles away, who never traveled to America. Hmm . . . the mystery grows.

Sequoyah and Sequoia

Meanwhile, back in the redwoods' original habitat (Oregon to California), the Native people have many names for the trees. The Tule River Tribe calls them *Toos-pung-ish, Hea-mi-withic*, the Ancient Ones, out of respect for the trees' height and age. The Monos call them *Wawona*, after the spirit owl that guards the giant trees. When non-Natives first saw them, some wanted to call them *Wellingtonia* and others *Washingtonia*, but sequoia was finally chosen.

So how to solve the mystery? What Sequoyah and Endlicher had in common was a love of words. It is believed that Endlicher learned about Sequoyah's syllabary and named the tree after him because Endlicher knew what a gigantic job creating a syllabary was. It made Sequoyah a giant among men, so it made sense to link him with the largest living plant. Today, there are two accepted spellings of the word: sequoia for the genus or family of trees and Sequoyah for the Cherokee word genius.

Ss Again!

(tuh-BOG-uhn)

From the Mi'kmaq, *topagan*
or the Passammaquody, *thapakan*
or the Anishinabe, *nobugidaban*
To English, toboggan

The sport of bobsledding is all about speed, ice, and the rush of adrenaline.

Bobsled teams are composed of either two or four men or women. They line up on both sides of the bobsled at the top of an icy raceway called a run. At a signal, they body slam themselves into the bobsled. The driver sits up straight in the front to pilot the run. The others crouch low to increase speed. Competition bobsleds careen downhill at speeds exceeding 90 miles per hour in an attempt to earn an Olympic medal. But there would be no extreme sport sleds like bobsleds, luges, or skeletons if not for the toboggan, an American Indian original, the ancestor of them all.

Native people from the north country of both the United States and Canada—the Mi'kmaq, Passamaquoddy, Innu, Cree, and Anishinabe, among others—developed the toboggan thousands of years ago to carry goods and people across lands that remain snow covered for most of the year.

The first toboggans were runnerless machines constructed from bark or animal hides. Later, they were made from long slats of wood held together by crosspieces. Heat or steam shaped the front ends up into the familiar J curve. Toboggans had a rope for steering and were pulled by either people or dogs. Today, many Native people still rely on toboggans, although they often power them with snowmobiles.

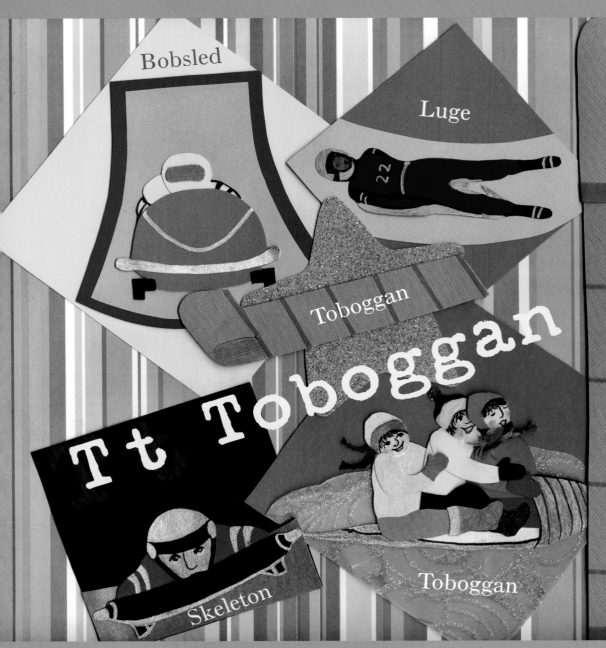

Bobsled

Luge

Toboggan

Tt Toboggan

Skeleton

Toboggan

Tobogganing is also fun! When you feel the need for winter speed, grab a toboggan, snow gear, some basic safety rules, and call your friends. Meet at the slopes, chutes, or a nearby hill to experience your own adrenaline rush.

(oo-koo-LEY-ley or yoo-koo-LEY-ley)

From Hawaiian, *ukulele*
To English, ukulele

In 1879 João Fernandes left his home on Madeira Island to work on a sugar plantation in Hawaii. The trip took four long months, and to pass the time Fernandes borrowed a guitarlike instrument, a *braginho*, from another passenger. A natural musician, Fernandes took to the miniguitar like cheese to pizza. When the ship finally reached Honolulu, Fernandes leapt onto the dock, thrilled to be on land again, and played an impromptu braginho concert of Portuguese songs.

The unique sound of the instrument was an instant hit with the Hawaiian people. Portable and easy to learn, many were eager for one. Manuel Nunes, who had traveled with Fernandes, was a skilled craftsman. He and others started companies to make enough instruments to meet the growing demand. Before long, the instrument was given a Hawaiian name, *ukulele*.

Some said ukulele means "jumping flea" because of the lightning speed of Fernandes' fingers as he plucked the ukulele's four strings. However, the last monarch of Hawaii, Queen Lili'uokalani, disagreed: she said it was a combination of two Hawaiian words: *uku*, meaning gift, and *lele*, meaning to come or "the gift that came here," which indeed it had.

Uu Ukulele

In the early 1900s the ukulele took the United States by storm. From there its popularity went global. Over time this small instrument has affected many different genres of music, from jazz to grunge rock, but it will always be associated with the beautiful Hawaiian Islands.

(vi-KOO-nuh)

From Quechua, *wik'uña*
To Spanish, *vicuña*
To English, vicuña

Capturing vicuñas, one of the planet's wildest animals, takes patience, sturdy corrals, and maybe 1,000 people standing together, yelling and singing. Huh?

Related to llamas (check out the L page), vicuñas live in the Andes Mountains of South America. They are tricky to catch for a few reasons. First, they live at the highest and hardest to reach elevations (11,000+ feet), places with few roads and less oxygen.

Vicuñas' temperament and speed also help them stay wild. Naturally shy, they have excellent hearing. When the alpha male of a herd hears anything unusual, he bleats an alarm. The herd runs away at speeds up to 30 miles per hour, leaving most humans in the dust. So why do people *want* to catch vicuñas? One word: wool.

The Inca were the original people of the Andes, but domesticated only alpacas and llamas. Every three years or so they would hold a *chacu*, or communal rounding up of vicuñas.

Hundreds of thousands of people would hold hands and encircle thousands of vicuñas, singing and yelling the animals towards stone corrals. Instead of butchering vicuñas, they would shear the wool and release the animals.

Vv Vicuña

Vicuña wool is the finest, warmest wool in the world, both then and now. Long ago only Inca kings and their families could wear garments spun from vicuña fleece. The punishment for anyone else was death. Gulp. Today, vicuña wool products come at a price as high as an Andean peak. A woman's scarf costs about $1,500 and a coat runs $20,000 or more. Gulp times 2!

By the 1960s vicuñas were endangered, but now Quechua villagers and governments protect the herds. In many places, the custom of chacu is being revived. People again join hands around the vicuñas, singing, capturing, shearing then releasing vicuñas, the wild spirit animals of the Andes.

(WOM-puhm)

From Massachusett and Narragansett, *wampumpeag*
To English, wampum

L ong ago, the Native peoples of the east coast collected, cut, and drilled the white, spiraled shells of the whelks and the purple eyespots of quahog shells (check out the Q page), into beads called *wampumpeag* or wampum.

Over time, wampum belts became more than jewelry. Messages were woven into the designs. The messages were memorized by men called Wampum Keepers, who had been trained from childhood to retell the stories within the wampum belts.

The *Haudenosaunee*, or Iroquois Confederation (the Mohawk, Cayuga, Seneca, Oneida, and the Onondaga nations, with the Tuscaroras joining later), say wampum was given to them thousands of years ago by a holy man known only as the Peacemaker and his follower, *Ayonwatha* or Hiawatha.

The Peacemaker asked warring nations to change. They would keep their own council fires, their ruling Chiefs and Clan Mothers, but in matters that affected all the nations they should act peacefully, with "one mind."

This new concept, that nations work best separately *and* in unison, was woven on a famous wampum belt known as the Hiawatha Belt, the original one as old as the Iroquois Confederacy itself. The heart-shaped symbol in the center represents the Great Tree of Peace or the central nation, the Onondaga. The four white squares represent the other member nations. The Hiawatha Belt's opening words, "We the People . . ." influenced Benjamin Franklin and Thomas Jefferson, who penned those words into the preamble of the United States' Constitution.

Ww Wampum

(KHAHT)

From Haida, *xat*
To English, xat

Carved from gigantic red cedar trees, totem poles honor Pacific Northwest Indian families and greet visitors, rising 30 to 60 feet above coastal village homes. Each carved and painted crest image tells clan membership and wonderful stories: of Raven, who brought light and salmon to the world; of Thunderbird, who ruled the skies and the weather; of Wolf, who stood for cunning and wisdom on land; of Grizzly Bear, who represented fierce power; and of Killer Whale, who was the spirit of the seas.

There are four types of totem poles used for different reasons. A xat is a mortuary pole, used originally as a tomb. Its hollowed out back or rectangular top frontal board held the remains of a deceased person. In time, nature would weather the xat enough to return to the earth. Although xats are no longer used this way, modern Native artists continue to create totem poles, a unique style of art found nowhere else on earth.

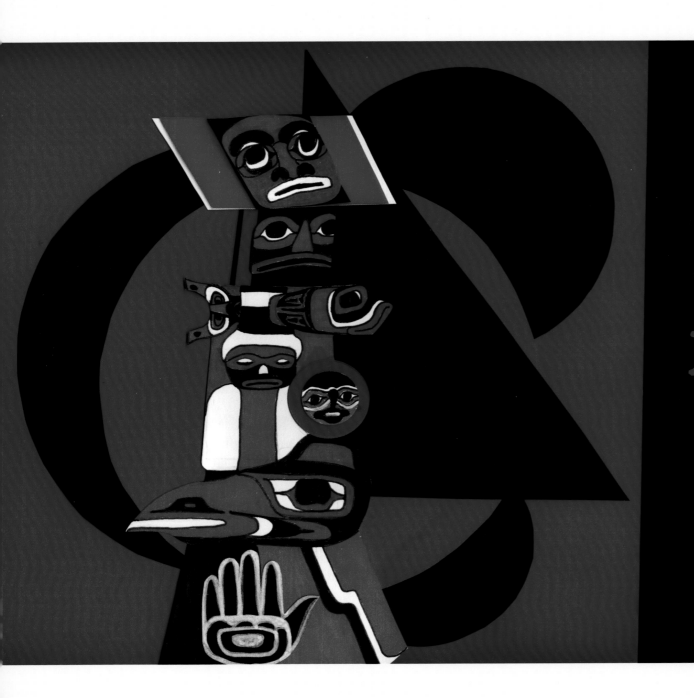

Xx

Xat

(YUHK-uh)

From Taino, *yuka*
(EE-u-kah)
To English, yuca

Of all the weirdly wonderful things in the world, the yuca plant, also known as cassava or manioc, should rank in the top ten. The Taino word, *yuka*, comes from *Yukahu*, spirit of the sun, the breath of the Creator, which shows how much they respected this vital, yet tricky plant.

Like potatoes, cassava plants produce underground tubers with a tough brown skin, but here's the tricky part: when exposed to the air, the tubers chemically become poisonous. Thousands of years ago Native people of South America experimented with this weird gift of nature. Though we may never know exactly how they figured out the process of detoxifying yuca, their methods were passed through families and over trade routes to the Caribbean islands and ultimately to the world.

For yuca tubers to be safely eaten, they must be peeled, chopped, or grated, then soaked in water.

Yy

After squeezing out the water, the yuca can be baked, roasted, or dried and ground into a flour to make many foods from soups and breads to cakes and tapioca pudding.

Today, people around the world depend on yuca, the woody shrub that has given people a dangerous, but nutritious, food.

Yuca

(ZOH-pee-lote)

From Nahuatl (Aztec), *tzopilotl*
To Spanish, *zopilote*
To English, zopilote

To the Aztecs, the twelfth-century rulers of Mexico, the vulture symbolized long life, which is definitely true for the zopilote, or the American Black Vulture. Fossil remains of a prehistoric zopilote species prove they have existed for about 9,000 years. Consequently, they have learned some weird, but wonderful ways to adapt.

Black Vultures often cannot feed every day, so their bodies metabolize, or burn fat, slowly. The downside of this is that their bodies are slow to warm up. In the early morning, the vultures stretch both wings to their full span of five feet. Are they hoping for a group hug? No way! They wing stretch to gather warmth and make the best use of sunlight.

A Weird Eww! Fact: Like all scavengers, Black Vultures eat carrion or animal carcasses. Scavengers have a bad reputation despite the vital job they do ridding the world of decaying things. To the scavenger, carrion is an easy and nutritious source of food that requires no hunting, but the trick is to locate it.

Dead bodies release chemicals and bacteria that broadcast a stink alarm. This, in turn, alerts scavengers to food sources. However, Black Vultures have almost no sense of smell, so again they have adapted. A related species, the Turkey Vulture, has a keen sense of smell and prefers to forage alone. Black

Vultures hunt in colonies, often trailing a Turkey Vulture. When a Turkey Vulture finds carrion, it lands and starts to feed. The Black Vultures force it aside so they feed first. By human standards this system may not seem fair, but it works for the vultures.

Zz Zopilote

Weird & Wonderful Facts, a.k.a., the Bibliography

Instead of a formal bibliography, I have written a fun version, spliced with extra cool facts and my acknowledgments. I did a plethora of research for this book. My #1 source is a great book: *O Brave New Words* by Charles L. Cutler (University of Oklahoma Press, 1994). My other major source was the Internet. I googled myself silly on each of my words and of course, one site led to another, too many to list. The ones I relied on most were www.native-languages.org, www.wikipedia.org, and www.dictionary.com.

Abalone

What makes abalone shells extra strong? Using microscopes, some scientists discovered the shells are composed of calcium carbonate tiles, arranged like tiny bricks with a protein substance underneath like mortar. When the shell is struck, the tiles slide and the "mortar" absorbs the blow. The scientists are developing new types of body armor based on this. A special thanks goes to my local "Shell Lady," Lisa Ross, for her expertise. Thanks also to Louise Ramirez who talked with me about abalone from the Native Californian perspective. For abalone science facts, check out www.abalonenetwork.org and click SCIENCE.

Barbecue

The Hearth, Patio & Barbecue Association (HPBA) has declared May as National Barbecue Month because a. they need to promote their industry and b. mostly to enjoy the 4Fs of food, family, friends, and fun, . . . and that rocks!

Canoe

Whether alive or fallen, the giant western red cedar trees were homes to zillions of bird and animal species. After being carved into canoes, the trees then became the perfect link between land and sea, and people, plants, and animals.

Special, special thanks goes to my author friend, Philip Red Eagle, who shared his wealth of knowledge and experience of canoe clubs with me. Check out www.nativeartists.org and click on The Gift Canoe Project. To learn more about Northwest Pacific canoe clubs visit http://tribaljourneys.wordpress.com or www.canoeway.org. A special thanks goes to Robert Steelquist, the education coordinator at the Olympic Coast National Marine Sanctuary.

Dowitcher

Dowitchers eat mollusks and crustaceans by poking their bills into the mud up-and-down, up-and-down, faster than Sonic the Hedgehog can zoom. They capture and swallow their food under the mud, except for worms. For reasons known only to dowitchers, worms are pulled to the surface first and then eaten.

Eulachon

Scott Byram and David Lewis, two University of Oregon researchers, wrote a scholarly article titled "Ourigan: Wealth of the Northwest Coast" (*Oregon Historical Quarterly*, Summer 2001). It said that by the 1700s, some trading routes were known as the Grease Trails because the primary trade item was eulachon oil. These trails earned the name because people living far from the coasts desired oil from ooligan-eulachon-ourigan-or-whatever-other-name-you-choose for the tiny fish. The Grease Trails extended from Alaska to the Fraser River and even as far as the Rocky Mountains. Check out www.ohs.org, the Oregon History Project's website (http://www.ohs.org/education/oregonhistory/). The Grease Trails also jump-started a language, Chinook Jargon. Check out www.nativelanguages.org.

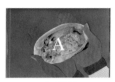

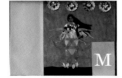

Fanilusa Bayou

This obscure bayou is located in rural Louisiana. I live in rural California and would not have found any information on it if not for the Internet and the wonderful efforts of a dedicated librarian, Doris Lively, who works at Grant Parish Library in Louisiana, and her husband. Many thanks!

Geoduck

Scientists tell a geoduck's age by counting the markings on its shell the way botanists count rings on a tree. The humble geoduck is also the mascot of Evergreen State College in Olympia, Washington, even though they do not have a football team.

Hooghan

Excellent information on the hooghan can be found at the website www.hanksville.org, or from a small book, *The Hogan*, by Scott Thybony, published by Western National Parks Association, Tuscon, Arizona, in 1999.

Iguana

Green iguanas have a weird "third eye" on top of their heads. Its scientific name is a parietal eye, but it is not used for seeing. Instead, it warns of movement from above—for example, sneaky predators. Plus it helps the iguana sense when it has absorbed enough sunlight, a cool "tool" for a cold-blooded animal to have. Depending on where they live, green iguanas may also be red, lavender, black, orange, or pink. Young iguanas may be bright green or blue, but these colors fade as the animal ages.

Jaguar

Jaguars enjoy the water and frequently swim following prey. More weirdly wonderful, a jaguar will often wait along a riverbank, every so often flicking the water's surface with its tail. The movement lures fish to jump and zzzzap! . . . jaguar lunch! Read more jaguar facts at www.zoo.org.

Kinnikinnik

The word kinnikinnik is a palindrome, a word spelled the same way back to front or front to back. It is the longest palindrome in the English language, something else the animals that depend on it do not care about.

Llama

Llamas hum, but not to audition for *American Idol*. They hum when tired, uncomfortable, or curious. Breeders say the humming ranges from shrill to mellow depending on the llama's reason. The best weirdly wonderful reason llamas hum is when a dam (a female) gives birth to a cria (baby). If in a herd, other females surround the dam and hum, too, until the cria is born. For more information about llamas, visit www.llamaweb.com.

Maize

An important product of maize, or corn, is corn syrup, a sweetener used in many products and also used as "blood." Huh? Corn syrup holds moisture for a long time, so some movie special effects people add red dye to corn syrup. This "blood" looks real and does not dry quickly, even during long filming sessions.

Thanks should be given to scientists around the world for producing thousands of products we use every day, all from maize and its varied by-products: aspirin, soft drinks, cereal, toothpaste, glue, tortillas, paper plates, car and bike tires, to name a few. It is estimated that of 10,000 items in a large food store, over 2,000 of them have some form of corn, or maize. A great book is *The Story of Corn* by Betty Harper Fussell (North Point Press/Farrar, Straus & Giroux, 1992).

Nēnē

The Hawaiian archipelago is a 1,500-mile string of islands created by undersea volcanoes in the middle of the Pacific Ocean, far from any continents. This isolation means all native plants and animals arrived by one of the "Three Ws": waves, ocean currents; wind, on the air; or wings, birds, insects, and what they carried. Thousands of years ago one winged arrival was the Canada goose. Its modern descendants are the Nēnē, the world's most rare geese. An awesome book is *Nēnē* by my author friend Marion Coste (University of Hawaii Press, Honolulu, 1993).

Opossum

Opossums have been in existence for 70 or 80 *million* years! When threatened, opossums not only play dead, but have other survival adaptations, including a few *Ewww!* ones: they hiss, growl, belch, urinate, or defecate.

Pogonip

This picture is of a real tree iced by a real pogonip in 2005 in the really cool state of Nevada. It was taken by my author friend Suzanne Morgan Williams. Check out her website, www.suzannebooks.com.

Quahog

Many of my friends who read *Giveaways* while it was a work in progress were delighted to see the Q page word, quahog, because they expected to read about the fictional town of Quahog from the Fox animated series *Family Guy*. They were dismayed to be reading about a clam. For more quahog information, go to http://www.quahog.com and click on "About the Quahog."

Raccoon

Raccoons are wild animals with quick tempers, known to bite when handled, which is why I did not create a cutesy illustration. Besides the chance of causing rabies, raccoons pass parasites called roundworms through their bodily wastes. Roundworms and their eggs may stay in the soil for years. Always wash your hands after being outside to avoid infections.

Skunk

Like many characters from the Stephenie Meyer's *Twilight* series, skunks are crepuscular. No, they are not vampires; crepuscular means to be mostly active at dawn and dusk. SKUNK is also a fun classroom math game invented by Dan Brutlag. To find out more, go to http://illuminations.nctm.org/LessonDetail.aspx?id=L248.

Sequoyah & Sequoia

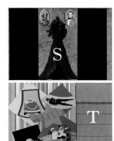

Tons of information can be found on both the man and the tree in books and online. One of my favorite sources is the picture book entitled *Sequoyah, The Cherokee Man Who Gave His People Writing* by James Rumford (Houghton Mifflin Company, 2004). The best thing about this book is: The author is another of my friends? No. His beautiful art? No. His wonderful words? No. All the cool back matter? No. The combination of English and Cherokee words on each page? **YES!** Anna Sixkiller Huckaby did all the Cherokee translations. Special thanks also goes to MariJo Moore for her advice, www.marijomoore.com.

Toboggan

Everyone agrees this popular winter sport was invented in the late 1800s in Switzerland, but who deserves the credit? Was it an American tourist on vacation in Switzerland, a few American and British tourists together, or the Swiss themselves? No one knows, but most bobsled teams do not seem concerned. BTW: only Americans call the bobsled a bobsled. People from other countries call them bob*sleighs*.

An awesome book: *Bobsledding & the Luge: A True Book* by Larry Dane Brimner (Children's Press, a division of Grolier Publishers, New York, 1997).

Ukulele

I made the background for this page from Black Magic paper from www.coredinations.com. I scratched away the designs instead of cutting pictures from paper as I did for the other pages. I did this because I wanted the background to resemble Hawaiian *kapa* (*tapa*) cloth, made from the pounded bark of the *wauke* or *po'a'aha* paper mulberry trees or the *mamaki* tree. To read more, visit www.eastmauiwatershed.org/Plants.

Vicuña

Vicuña wool is the most rare in the world because the animals produce only about a pound of fleece per shearing, as compared to sheep, which yield between 12 and 20 pounds. Plus, vicuñas' wool grows slowly and they can be shorn only once every three or four years.

Wampum

According to the *American Heritage Dictionary*, one meaning of the word book is "something regarded as a source of knowledge or understanding." In this sense, wampum belts should be considered one of the world's first types of books. Besides the sacred meaning of wampum described on the W page, American Indians used wampum belts and strings primarily for diplomatic purposes, helping nations come to peaceful agreements. After Europeans settled in America, they were at a loss for currency, so for them wampum became money. Soon, factories were started to mass-produce it. According to www.us-coin-values-advisor.com in its section on the history of U.S. coins, wampum in the colonial period could be used to pay your Commonwealth of

Massachusetts taxes or Harvard University tuition. For more information, read *Wampum Belts of the Iroquois* by Ray Fadden Tehanetorens (Summertown, Tennessee: Book Publishing Co., 1999).

Xat

Besides the xat, there are three other types of totem poles: interior house poles to support the house structure; frontal poles placed in front of a house, often as the actual door; memorial poles to honor an event or a famous person. Totem poles were never religious or witchcraft symbols, but are similar to a coat of arms or a billboard ad. One of the most well-known xats was built to honor Chief Skedans, who lived in the Haida village of Skidegate on Queen Charlotte Islands, British Columbia. The original pole, carved before 1878, was moved to Vancouver, British Columbia, in 1936, and displayed in Stanley Park. It remained there until it decayed due to the sea climate. In 1964 a famous Haida artist, Bill Reid, and his assistant, Werner True, made an exact replica of the Skedans pole. Its moonface top had to be recarved in 1998 by Don Yeomans. It stands in the Totem Park section of Vancouver, British Columbia's Stanley Park, www.seestanleypark.com.

Yuca

Columbus and his men were amazed at the process the Taino people had developed to remove toxins from yuca and make it safe to eat (peel, grate, soak, squeeze, then cook). He took some yuca back to Spain, described the process, and impressed the court. Thanks goes to Mukaro Agueibana, the current president of the United Confederation of Taino People, for help with all the Taino words in my book. According to him, the word yuca comes from the spirit name for the sun. FYI: He is helping to standardize the spelling of the Taino language and prefers the spelling yuka to distinguish it further from the agave plant, yucca. To see the insignia of the United Confederation of Taino People flag, designed by Marie "Nana" Crooke, go to The Voice of the Taino People Online, at www.uctp.blogspot.com.

Zopilote

As twilight falls at Gettysburg National Military Park in Pennsylvania, Black Vultures return to roost like their ancestors have done for the last 146 years. From July 1–3, 1863, 50,000 men were killed on this land in one of the bloodiest battles of the American Civil War. Both Union and Confederate armies took care of their fallen soldiers, but they had to abandon thousands of dead horses. Thousands of Black Vultures arrived, silent as the empty battlefields, and set to work cleaning what humans could not. From that day on, Black Vultures have perched in the trees of the Gettysburg Park, grim reminders of a troubled past. An awesome YouTube video: "Vultures of Getty," produced by WPSU, Penn State Public Broadcasting.